LEADERS LIKE US
Pauli Mu[rray]

BY KAITLYN DULING

ILLUSTRATED BY ARVILLA MAE MORETT

Rourke™

Before Reading: *Building Background Knowledge and Vocabulary*

Building background knowledge can help children process new information and build upon what they already know. Before reading a book, it is important to tap into what children already know about the topic. This will help them develop their vocabulary and increase their reading comprehension.

Questions and Activities to Build Background Knowledge:

1. Look at the front cover of the book and read the title. What do you think this book will be about?
2. What do you already know about this topic?
3. Take a book walk and skim the pages. Look at the table of contents, photographs, captions, and bold words. Did these text features give you any information or predictions about what you will read in this book?

Vocabulary: *Vocabulary Is Key to Reading Comprehension*

Use the following directions to prompt a conversation about each word.

- Read the vocabulary words.
- What comes to mind when you see each word?
- What do you think each word means?

Vocabulary Words:
- autobiography
- civil rights
- feminism
- gender
- priest
- pronouns
- protest
- segregated

During Reading: *Reading for Meaning and Understanding*

To achieve deep comprehension of a book, children are encouraged to use close reading strategies. During reading, it is important to have children stop and make connections. These connections result in deeper analysis and understanding of a book.

 Close Reading a Text

During reading, have children stop and talk about the following:

- Any confusing parts
- Any unknown words
- Text to text, text to self, text to world connections
- The main idea in each chapter or heading

Encourage children to use context clues to determine the meaning of any unknown words. These strategies will help children learn to analyze the text more thoroughly as they read.

When you are finished reading this book, turn to the next-to-last page for **Text-Dependent Questions** and an **Extension Activity**.

TABLE OF CONTENTS

WORDS HAVE POWER

Have you ever sat down to create something and forgotten to stop? Have you ever written all day long? Or maybe painted, played basketball, or danced? The Rev. Dr. Pauli Murray knew that feeling. Pauli loved to write. Once the keys of the typewriter started clacking, there was no stopping Pauli.

"Click. Click. Clack." Pauli typed the final few letters. The paper pulled smoothly from the typewriter. Then it went, folded, into an envelope. Pauli was sending another letter to the president. Those words would help Pauli change the country for the better. From **civil rights** to **gender** equality, Pauli Murray was leading the way. With one typewriter and a stack of papers, Pauli was writing the future.

FIGHTING FOR CHANGE

Pauli Murray was born in 1910. Pauli's parents gave their child the name Anna Pauline. After Pauli's mother passed away, Pauli was sent to live with family members in Durham, North Carolina, including Aunt Pauline. The house had a wide front porch and a big yard. Pauli grew up there.

Life was hard for kids like Pauli. The schools in Durham were **segregated**. Pauli went to Hillside High School with other Black students. But Pauli didn't want to go to a segregated college. Instead, they went to Hunter College in New York City and studied English literature.

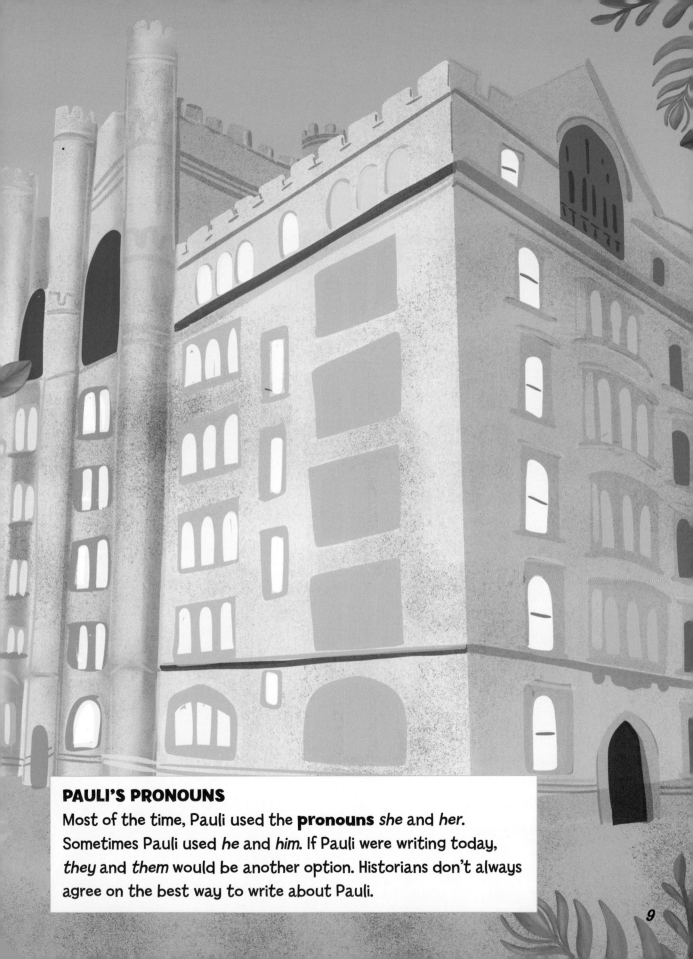

PAULI'S PRONOUNS

Most of the time, Pauli used the **pronouns** *she* and *her*.
Sometimes Pauli used *he* and *him*. If Pauli were writing today,
they and *them* would be another option. Historians don't always
agree on the best way to write about Pauli.

After graduating, Pauli worked as a teacher. Pauli also kept writing. Articles and poems of Pauli's were published in magazines such as *The Crisis*. Around this time, Pauli started using the name "Pauli" instead of "Anna."

Pauli never felt quite like a girl. Sometimes Pauli felt like a boy or felt in-between. Aunt Pauline lovingly called Pauli her "boy/girl." Pauli asked doctors if there was something wrong. But there wasn't. Pauli was just...Pauli!

Pauli had always loved to write and wanted to use words to change things for the better. In 1940, Pauli challenged segregation on a city bus in Virginia and was arrested.

Pauli continued to **protest**. Pauli wrote letters—lots of them! Some of those letters went to President Roosevelt. He didn't reply, but the first lady did. Over the years, Pauli and Eleanor Roosevelt became friends. They wrote letters back and forth for the rest of their lives. Pauli wrote about civil rights and **feminism**. Mrs. Roosevelt listened.

ELEANOR ROOSEVELT

Pauli decided to become a lawyer but was rejected from the University of North Carolina. The school did not accept Black students.

Instead, Pauli graduated from Howard University School of Law in Washington, DC. After that, Pauli applied to Harvard University to get a Master of Laws degree but was rejected once again. The school did not accept women.

Pauli kept going...
...kept writing letters...
...and kept fighting for what was right.

LOVE LETTERS

While working at a law firm, Pauli met a woman named Irene Barlow. Irene and Pauli wrote letters to one another. They fell in love. They were in love for many years, until Irene passed away.

WRITING THE FUTURE

Pauli kept writing: articles, essays, books. Slowly but surely, Pauli's words helped change the law.

In the 1960s, Pauli worked hard to make sure that the Civil Rights Movement helped men and women. In the 1970s, Pauli cofounded the National Organization for Women. Pauli's writing helped win cases about segregation, civil rights, and marriage equality.

PAULI THE POET

Pauli wasn't just a writer of law and books. Pauli was also a poet. Pauli's most famous poem, "Dark Testament," weaves words into stories of slavery and segregation. It imagines a more equal world.

Later on in life, Pauli became a **priest**. It was a big step. A Black woman had never been a priest in the Episcopal Church before. Even though Pauli didn't always feel like a woman, that's how Pauli was understood by many other people.

Pauli's first service was performed at the Chapel of the Cross in Chapel Hill, North Carolina. Pauli's grandmother, an enslaved woman, had been baptized there. This was an important moment for Pauli.

Pauli lived a long and very full life. In the 1980s, Pauli put the finishing touches on an **autobiography**. Pauli's office was full of books, files, and stacks and stacks of paper. Pauli wrote everything down. In 1985, Pauli passed away in Pittsburgh, Pennsylvania. But Pauli's words and ideas weren't forgotten.

Today, Pauli continues to be a role model for people of all genders, and especially for anyone who knows that words have the power to change the world.

> " One person plus one typewriter constitutes a movement.
>
> –Pauli Murray

TIME LINE

1910   Pauli Murray is born in Baltimore, Maryland, to Agnes and William Murray.

1933   Pauli graduates from Hunter College in New York City.

1940   15 years before Rosa Parks refuses to move, Pauli is arrested for protesting segregation on Virginia buses.

1944   Pauli graduates at the top of their law school class from Howard University in Washington, DC.

1944   Pauli takes part in a sit-in at a Washington, DC, cafeteria.

1956   Pauli's first book, *Proud Shoes: The Story of an American Family* is published.

1965   Pauli is the first Black student awarded a law doctorate from Yale University.

1965–73 Pauli serves on the board of the American Civil Liberties Union.

1966   Pauli cofounds the National Organization for Women.

1973   Pauli's partner, Irene Barlow, passes away.

1977   Pauli performs a service at Chapel of the Cross in Chapel Hill, North Carolina, where Pauli's grandmother, an enslaved person, had been baptized.

1985   Pauli passes away from cancer in Pittsburgh, Pennsylvania.

1987   Pauli's autobiography is published.

2012   Pauli is named a saint in the Episcopal Church.

GLOSSARY

autobiography (aw-toh-bye-AH-gruh-fee): a book in which the author tells the story of their own life

civil rights (SIV-uhl rites): the individual rights that all members of a democratic society have that ensure freedom and equal treatment under law

feminism (FEM-uh-niz-uhm): the advocacy for the equality of women and the belief that women should have the same rights and opportunities as men

gender (JEN-dur): the traits, such as behavioral or cultural, that are typically associated with one sex

priest (preest): a member of the clergy who can lead services and perform rites in certain religions

pronouns (PROH-nouns): words that take the place of nouns

protest (PROH-test): demonstration or statement against something

segregated (SEG-ri-gate-id): to have kept people or things apart from the main group

INDEX

TEXT-DEPENDENT QUESTIONS

1. What types of things did Pauli write?
2. Who did Pauli live with during childhood?
3. What pronouns did Pauli use?
4. Why didn't Pauli want to go to college in North Carolina?
5. How did Pauli help change the country for the better?

EXTENSION ACTIVITY

Pauli Murray wasn't afraid to write letters to important people like the president. If you were to write a letter to the president, what would you say? Think about changes that could help make your country a better place. Write your own letter to the president or to another leader. If you feel brave, have an adult help you send it! You might just get a response.

ABOUT THE AUTHOR

Kaitlyn Duling believes in the power of words. They can help you change hearts and minds! Kaitlyn is a poet and author who grew up in Illinois. She now lives with her wife in Washington, DC. Kaitlyn has written more than 100 books for children and teens. She hopes her books will inspire readers to tell the truest, bravest, and most beautiful stories they can imagine.

ABOUT THE ILLUSTRATOR

Arvilla Mae Morett is an illustrator and artist focused on feminism, mental health, and animal rights. She loves exploring new mediums such as watercolor and gouache. Her adventurous spirit allows her to express ideas and educate through illustrations. When she isn't creating, you can find her spending time with her family or helping foster dogs.

© 2023 Rourke Educational Media

www.rourkebooks.com

PHOTO CREDITS: cover, page 1: Illustration based on photograph by Associated Press page 20: Associated Press

Quote source: Brita Belli. "Happy birthday, Pauli! Students celebrate the civil rights activist and trailblazer." Yale News, November 19, 2018: https://news.yale.edu/2018/11/19/happy-birthday-pauli-students-celebrate-activist-and-trailblazer

Edited by: Hailey Scragg
Illustrations by: Arvilla Mae Morett
Cover and interior layout by: J.J. Giddings

Library of Congress PCN Data

Pauli Murray / Kaitlyn Duling
(Leaders Like Us)
ISBN 978-1-73165-283-6 (hard cover)
ISBN 978-1-73165-253-9 (soft cover)
ISBN 978-1-73165-313-0 (e-book)
ISBN 978-1-73165-343-7 (e-pub)
Library of Congress Control Number: 2021952203

Rourke Educational Media
Printed in the United States of America
01-2412211937